Published by Bushel & Peck Books, a family-run publishing house in Fresno,
California, who believes in uplifting children with the highest standards of art, music,
literature, and ideas. For every book we sell, we donate one to a child in need—book for book.
To nominate a school or organization to receive free books, or to find inspiring books and gifts,
please visit www.bushelandpeckbooks.com.

ISBN: 978-1-63819-172-8   LCCN: 2023944642

First Edition

Printed in China

1 3 5 7 9 10 8 6 4 2

Type set in Bebas and Tipique.

SLEEP

A Kid's Guide to the Science of Slumber

Wendy Bjazevich

Illustrated by Juliana Eigner

BUSHEL
& PECK
BOOKS

Contents

1 What is sleep?

For many years, sleep was thought to be a time when a person's body and brain didn't do much of, well, anything. Today, because of research and study—much of it since the early 1950s—scientists know that this isn't true!

Experts have determined that sleep is not a passive activity. In fact, they have discovered that a *lot* goes on in both the body and the brain while sleep is occurring.

HOW DOES THE BODY REGULATE SLEEP?

Being awake during the day and sleeping at night is considered a hard-wired pattern for the human body. There are two main systems that help regulate sleep: a person's **homeostatic sleep drive** and **circadian rhythms**.

These two components work together to shape a person's sleep and wake times. Essentially, they determine how much the body feels like it *needs* to sleep.

HOMEOSTATIC SLEEP DRIVE

Your body wants sleep when it's tired, just like it wants food when it's hungry. This is the homeostatic sleep drive at work. The longer you're awake, the more the pressure—or "drive"—for sleep builds. This same drive decreases during sleep.

There are also certain circumstances, like demanding physical or mental activities (hello, school!), that can also produce an elevated drive for sleep.

BRAIN

SCN

CIRCADIAN RHYTHMS

Circadian rhythms can be thought of as the body's internal cycles. These rhythms last around twenty-four hours, and then they repeat. While circadian rhythms help regulate many important biological processes such as **hormone** levels, **metabolism**, and body temperature, the **sleep-wake cycle** is perhaps the most well-known rhythm.

Circadian rhythms are regulated by **biological clocks**. No, there's no ticking or tocking, but almost every organ and tissue *does* have an invisible natural timing device, and these are what we mean by clock.

In turn, biological clocks are coordinated by a **master clock**. This master clock is located in the **suprachiasmatic nucleus**, or SCN, which is in the brain.

How do clocks function? It varies, but when it comes to your sleep clock, it has a lot to do with light. When you are exposed to less light, the SCN tells the brain to make more **melatonin**, a hormone that helps you feel sleepy. When you are exposed to more light, the SCN tells the brain to make less melatonin, so you feel awake and alert.

② Riding the sleep cycle

The time you spend sleeping doesn't look the same throughout the night. During an average night of sleep, a person will typically progress through three to six different **sleep cycles**.

On average, each cycle lasts around 90 minutes, but they can range in time from 70 to 120 minutes. Age, stress, and sleep environment are just a few of the many factors that can impact sleep cycle length.

THE STAGES OF SLEEP

Each individual sleep cycle is made up of four sleep stages: Stage 1, Stage 2, Stage 3, and Stage 4. These four stages are based on the brain's activity during sleep. Each stage plays an important role in the cycle. The first three stages are classified as **Non-Rapid Eye Movement (NREM) sleep**, or non-REM sleep. Stage 4 is classified as **Rapid Eye Movement (REM) sleep**. Each stage is often identified by an alternate name or names. These names help to quickly clarify what type of sleep is occurring in that particular stage. Take a look below!

STAGE 1

TYPE: Non-REM; is often called N1

LENGTH: 1–5 minutes

STAGE 2

TYPE: Non-REM; is often called N2

LENGTH: 10–60 minutes long

STAGE 3

TYPE: Non-REM; is known by multiple names: N3, Delta Sleep, Slow-Wave Sleep (SWS), and Deep Sleep

LENGTH: 20–40 minutes

STAGE 4

TYPE: REM sleep

LENGTH: 10–60 minutes

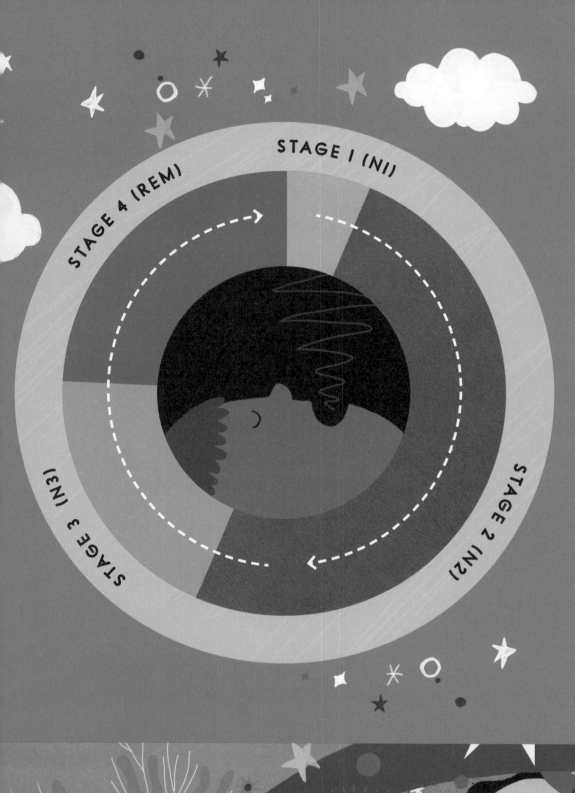

STAGE 4 (REM)

STAGE 1 (N1)

STAGE 2 (N2)

STAGE 3 (N3)

Sleep begins with N1 then progresses through N2, N3, and finally REM. After that, the sleep cycle starts all over again.

The length of sleep cycles also typically changes throughout the night. Normally the first sleep cycle of the evening is the shortest and later cycles are longer.

The typical length of time spent in each stage of a cycle also changes as you sleep. In the first sleep cycles of the evening, you spend more time in the non-REM sleep stages.

The length of REM sleep typically gets longer as the night progresses, with most REM sleep happening in the last half of the night. REM sleep stages tend to get longer and the N3 sleep stage shorter with every new sleep cycle.

WHAT IS NON-REM SLEEP?

During all three stages of non-REM sleep, a person's eyes are either relatively still or do not move. Here are some other things that happen (or don't happen!):

- A person's brain becomes less responsive to outside stimuli as it progresses from N1 to N3.
- It is less common for people to dream during non-REM sleep, though it can occur.

3 The four stages of sleep

The three non-REM sleep stages occur first in a person's sleep cycle and make up the largest part of the cycle. Approximately 5% of the sleep cycle is spent in N1, 45% in N2, and roughly 25% in N3. This leaves about 25% of the sleep cycle spent in REM sleep. While experts know that getting *enough* sleep is essential, they have also discovered that the time spent in each sleeping stage and the quality of that sleep is likewise significant. A healthy sleep cycle appears to rotate successfully through all four stages.

STAGE 1 (N1)

N1 starts the sleep cycle and is known as the "dozing off" stage. It is the transition period between being awake and being asleep. A person in **N1** sleep has their eyes closed, but they can be easily awakened. Both body and brain activity begins to slow down during this stage. N1 sleep is considered the lightest stage of sleep.

STAGE 2 (N2)

N2 sleep is considered a lighter type of sleep, but it's not as light as N1—the transition toward deep sleep is progressing in this stage. Both the body and the brain are continuing their slowdown, and it is still somewhat easy to wake up someone in N2 sleep. Unique types of brain activity can sometimes be seen during N2 sleep. On average, almost half of a person's sleep is spent in the N2 stage.

STAGE 3 (N3)

N3 is recognized as the deepest and most restorative stage of sleep. People in N3 sleep are the most difficult to wake up, and when they are awakened, they will often feel disoriented and groggy. Body and brain activity are at their slowest during this sleep stage. N3 sleep is a critical stage, according to scientists, for regenerating both body and brain. Sleepwalking can also occur during N3 sleep (see page 25).

STAGE 4 (REM)

The final and most active stage of the sleep cycle is REM sleep. Rapid Eye Movement Sleep got its name because of how a person's eyes quickly dart back and forth underneath their eyelids while they are asleep in this stage. During REM sleep, the brain is very active. Most dreaming occurs during REM sleep, and because of its high level of brain activity, the most intense and vivid dreams are associated with this stage.

4 What happens to our bodies during sleep?

While the body may appear to be completely inactive during sleep, research has shown that it is not! During each stage of the sleep cycle, the body (including the brain, one of the body's very special organs) is experiencing change. In fact, there's a lot going on in the body while it sleeps.

STAGE 1 (N1)

During this stage the muscles remain active, but they begin to move from an alert state to a relaxed state. Brain waves, breathing, eye movements, and heart rate all begin to slow down. People in N1 sleep can sometimes experience a sudden muscle contraction, twitch, or even the feeling of falling! This common motion is called a **hypnic jerk** and, fortunately, is not dangerous.

BRAIN WAVES
CALM DOWN

EYE MOVEMENT
SLOWS

HEART RATE
DECREASES

BREATHING
SLOWS

MUSCLES SHIFT
FROM AN ALERT
STATE TO A
RELAXED STATE, BUT
REMAIN ACTIVE

HYPNIC JERKS
ARE COMMON

STAGE 2 (N2)

In N2 sleep, eye movements stop and brain waves, breathing, and heart rate all slow even further. Your body temperature also decreases in N2.

BRAIN ACTIVITY SLOWS FURTHER, BUT WITH OCASSIONAL QUICK BURSTS OF ACTIVITY

EYE MOVEMENT STOPS

BODY TEMPERATURE DECREASES

BREATHING SLOWS EVEN FURTHER

HEART RATE DECREASES EVEN FURTHER

BRAIN BURSTS

Though brain activity slows during N2, researchers have discovered that bursts of activity still happen. It's possible that this activity actually helps to prevent you from being woken up by other activity around you. Clever!

STAGE 3 (N3)

Stage 3 is the deepest sleep state. There is no eye movement, and your brain waves, breathing, heart rate, and muscle activity are all at their slowest.

Delta brain waves are produced during N3 sleep. These brain waves are slow waves. During slow wave sleep, the body relaxes even further, resulting in a state of deep, **restorative** sleep. *Ahhhhhh.*

Not only is energy restored in this stage, but this is when **cell regeneration** occurs. From tissue to muscle to bone, your body performs many repair jobs during this phase. N3 sleep is even associated with boosting the immune system.

Even better, N3's deep sleep is also thought to play an important part in certain brain functions, like memory and effective thinking. That's why getting a good night's sleep is so important to doing well in school!

GROWTH SPURT

Though you have growth hormones working all day, it is at night, during the N3 stage, that the most intense period of growth hormone release occurs. According to researchers, when kids don't consistently get enough sleep, their growth could be slowed or stunted.

DELTA WAVES RELAX THE BODY TO ITS DEEPEST STATE

ENHANCES MEMORY AND EFFECTIVE THINKING

CELL REGENERATION OCCURS

TISSUE, MUSCLE, AND BONE GROW AND ARE REPAIRED

STAGE 4 (REM)

REM sleep is not considered a restful stage of sleep. Rather, it is the brain's most active sleep stage and the primary stage for dreaming (see page 22). Eye movements become rapid during the REM stage. Your body temperature rises, as does an increase in breathing, heart rate, and brain activity.

BRAIN IS MOST ACTIVE

BREATHING INCREASES

DREAMING OCCURS

TEMPERATURE INCREASES

HEART RATE INCREASES

MANY MUSCLES BECOME TEMPORARILY IMMOBILE

BODY BIND

During REM sleep, your muscles might experience temporary **paralysis.** When this happens, your body becomes temporarily immobile, except for the eyes and the breathing muscles.

5 Is sleep important?

Human beings spend about one-third of their life sleeping. That is a lot of time! For decades, scientists have questioned and examined if getting so much sleep was *really* necessary. While experts still don't have all the answers, one fact they do know for certain is that sleep is not only important, it is essential to life! In fact, sleeping is as necessary as food and water for you to survive and thrive.

JUST FIVE MORE MINUTES

Did you know? Human beings are the only mammals that can and will delay sleep when their body tells them it needs sleep.

THE BENEFITS OF SLEEP

Your physical, mental, and emotional health are all impacted by sleep. Some of the most noted potential benefits of sleep include:

Help in staying healthy and fighting against disease

Removal of brain cell waste

Increased capacity to concentrate, learn, and remember

Improved mood, judgment, motivation, and happiness

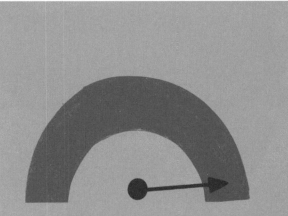

Reduced health risks

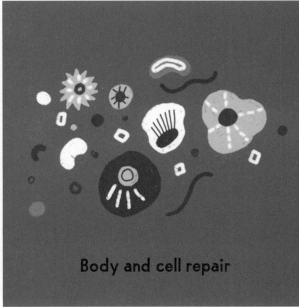

Body and cell repair

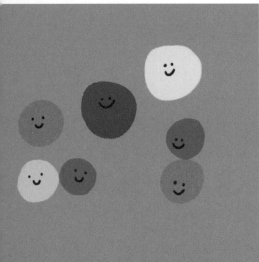

Body and cell growth

Better metabolism

So there you have it! The world of sleep is filled with many unanswered questions and mysteries. While the exact physiological roles of sleep are still uncertain, researchers are confident that the body does a lot of valuable work while sleeping.

6 How long do people need to sleep?

How much sleep a person needs can be influenced by many factors such as age, health, **genetics**, daytime activity level, and lifestyle habits.

THE AGE QUESTION

How much sleep you need mostly centers on your age. The amount of sleep a person requires changes as they get older. According to doctors, there is a range for each age group with a minimum and maximum number of hours recommended. Where do you fall on the scale?

NEWBORN BABIES

14–17 hours of sleep a day

INFANTS

12–16 hours of sleep a day (including naps)

TODDLERS

11–14 hours of sleep a day (including naps)

PRESCHOOL KIDS

10–13 hours of sleep a day (including naps)

CAN YOU SLEEP TOO MUCH?

Though getting enough sleep is essential to your health, it's also possible to sleep too much. While more research is needed, oversleeping has been linked to problems like **diabetes** and **obesity**—some of the same problems that happen with too *little* sleep!

NAPS

Love them or hate them, the research is clear: Naps can benefit all ages! Some of the positives include feeling refreshed and energized, increased creativity, brightened mood, decreased stress, heightened alertness, and improved memory. No wonder that, in some countries, taking a midday nap is considered a cultural tradition. However, the ideal nap shouldn't be too long. According to research, napping longer than about 30 minutes late in the afternoon can throw off your sleep schedule.

SCHOOL-AGE KIDS

9–12 hours of sleep a day

TEENS

8–10 hours of sleep a day

ADULTS

7–9 hours of sleep a day

ADULTS 65+

7–8 hours of sleep a day

7 Sleep hygiene

Sleep hygiene refers to a set of conditions and habits that can influence your nighttime sleep. Good **sleep hygiene** can help signal to the body that it's time to go to sleep. It can also help the body to sleep better.

FALLING ASLEEP

There are many healthy sleep practices, but some of the most important ones include:

HAVING A REGULAR BEDTIME SCHEDULE, even on holidays and weekends. This means going to bed and waking up around the same time each day.

FOLLOWING A CALMING BEDTIME ROUTINE. Doing the same thing every night, like taking a bath, putting on pajamas, or reading a book, can help your mind and your body feel more tired and ready for bed.

GETTING COZY! Turn down the lights, minimize noise, and make sure the room temperature is comfortable.

EXERCISING DURING THE DAY. Exercise and a little sunlight throughout the day may improve and promote sleep.

SLEEP DISTURBANCES

You also want to avoid things that might make sleeping more difficult, such as:

CAFFEINATED BEVERAGES like sodas and energy drinks late in the day. Caffeine is a **stimulant** and can make it harder to fall asleep.

ELECTRONICS like phones and computers can negatively affect sleep if used too close to bedtime. Experts recommend turning off all screens an hour or so before bedtime.

LONG NAPS LATE IN THE DAY can undermine a regular bedtime.

DAYTIME ACTIVITIES LIKE, HOMEWORK, GAMES, AND WATCHING TV IN BED. Sleeping will be easier if your mind connects your bed with sleep. Your bed should only be used for sleeping!

8 Dreams, dreams, dreams

Whether you remember them or not, experts say that everyone dreams. In fact, people may spend more than two hours each night dreaming. While you can dream in any stage of sleep, the most vivid, complex, and intense dreams take place during REM sleep.

WHY DO WE DREAM?

Scientists' understanding of dreaming has evolved over time, and while they still aren't exactly sure *why* people dream, they are developing curious theories about dreaming. Research suggests that dreaming may play an important part in forming memories and in learning. It may also have a role in managing stress responses and processing emotions.

BLACK AND WHITE TELEVISION

Studies have indicated that some people may dream in black and white instead of color. Scientists aren't certain why.

WHY DO WE FORGET DREAMS?

The reason people don't remember their dreams, or at least quickly forget them right after they wake up, isn't completely understood. One theory suggests this happens because the brain simply doesn't think dreams are important. Another theory suggests that a part of the brain called the **hippocampus** isn't fully awake when a person gets up, and this prevents you from retaining the dream's memory.

DREAM JOURNALS

If you want to remember more of your dreams, keep a dream journal! Write down your dreams as soon as you wake up.

NIGHTMARES

Most people have experienced a bad dream, or nightmare. In fact, medical experts regard these types of dreams as a common part of growing up.

What do nightmares mean? Well, it turns out that studying bad dreams is tricky. For one thing, the content of nightmares is random—there is no "usual" nightmare. And fear isn't the only emotion that can be involved in a nightmare. Sadness, stress, anger, and regret can also be felt.

What we *do* know is that nightmares seem to occur more commonly during REM sleep. They are also more likely to occur when you're overtired, depressed, anxious, stressed, or experiencing large life events.

Sleep disorders

A sleep disorder is a condition that can affect the timing of sleep, the quality of sleep, or the amount of sleep a person experiences. Sleep disorders can negatively impact a person's ability to function well in daily life.

Researchers have identified more than 100 sleep disorders, and millions of people experience some type of sleep disorder every year. Here are a few examples:

INSOMNIA

Perhaps the most common sleeping disorder is **insomnia**. People with this disorder can have trouble falling asleep, staying asleep, or a combination of both, and it can make them feel tired and sleepy during the day. In kids, insomnia can be caused by poor sleep hygiene (see page 20), caffeine consumption, medical issues, or stress.

SNORING

People may snore when air can't freely flow through the airway in their throat. Almost everyone snores occasionally, even children. Intense or regular snoring might signal a breathing disturbance.

SLEEP APNEA

Sleep apnea is a condition that causes a person to temporarily stop breathing while they are sleeping. There are two types of sleep apnea: **obstructive sleep apnea** (OSA) and **central sleep apnea** (CSA). OSA is the most common and occurs when soft tissue blocks the airway. CSA occurs when the brain stops signaling the muscles that control breathing to work. Sleep apnea can be treated with special breathing machines that keep air flowing all night.

NARCOLEPSY

In **narcolepsy**, the brain doesn't regulate the wake and sleep cycles correctly. Despite sleeping enough at night, people with narcolepsy can still feel exhausted during the day and may experience "**sleep attacks**" where they suddenly fall asleep. These attacks can last for a few seconds or even longer, sometimes for more than 30 minutes. Fortunately, narcolepsy is not common in kids.

RESTLESS LEG SYNDROME (RLS)

RLS can make it very difficult to sleep because of an almost uncontrollable urge to move one's legs. There might also be uncomfortable leg sensations like prickling, creeping, or tingling feelings. Generally, symptoms are used to identify RLS because doctors haven't yet found a specific test to diagnose it.

SLEEPWALKING

Sleepwalking is more common in kids than adults, and kids typically outgrow it by the time they are teenagers. Sleepwalking, also called **somnambulism**, usually happens an hour or two after a person falls asleep. Although a sleepwalker is asleep, their eyes will be open with a glazed or glassy appearance. While most people who sleepwalk get up and walk around, some just sit or stand in bed. People who sleepwalk usually won't remember anything they have done while sleepwalking. Scientists still don't know what causes sleepwalking, but it seems to run in families.

10 Weird sleep!

I'M FALLING!

Sometimes when you're falling asleep, or are in lighter sleep, you might experience a feeling of falling, a body twitch, or a jerk. This sudden movement might even wake you up! Some experts call these hypnic jerks. While researchers aren't sure what causes these movements, they're super common: Roughly 50% of people experience some type of jerk or twitch while sleeping.

NO NOSE KNOWS

Research has shown that your sense of smell decreases when you are asleep. Generally, smells or odors won't wake you up. (That's one reason smoke alarms are so important!)

CHATTY

While some people talk in their sleep, it is not uncommon for a deaf person to be seen using sign language in their sleep.

STUFF IT

Studies have shown numerous benefits related to sleeping with stuffed animals, including increased calmness, reduced stress, improved attachment, lessened loneliness, increased security, decreased anxiety, transitional benefits, and grief aid. In fact, scientists have concluded that there is no "right" age to stop sleeping with stuffed animals!

EYES WIDE OPEN

Yes! People can fall asleep with their eyes open (or partially open). This condition is called **nocturnal lagophthalmos**. Generally, people with this condition are unaware that their eyelids are not completely closed when they are sleeping. Adults, children, and even babies can experience nocturnal lagophthalmos. Having nocturnal lagophthalmos will not keep a person from going to sleep, but it can make sleep more restless. It may also cause eye problems.

II The bed

People have always wanted a comfortable place to sleep. In fact, archaeologists have found fossilized animal skins used as beds dating back to prehistoric times. What makes a bed has changed and evolved a lot since then.

Researchers discovered the oldest known mattress in South Africa. They estimate that it was created approximately 77,000 years ago! It was made of plant material and measured 22 square feet around and about 12 inches thick.

Egyptians are credited with raising beds off the ground. This helped people to escape the cold floor and avoid crawling, slithering creatures—*eeeek!* Other cultures used leaves, hay, cotton, feathers, and other materials to make and stuff beds. Later, the metal coil spring mattress was invented during the 19th century. Today, there are numerous mattress types that people can choose from. However, many cultures don't use mattresses at all. Take a look!

MATTRESS MAKEOVER

Unique beds can be found all over the world. Here are some of the ways people sleep:

HAMMOCK
(CENTRAL AND SOUTH AMERICA)

Hammocks are one of the oldest styles of beds. Typically, they are made of nylon rope or cotton and are suspended between two points. Hammocks allow for airflow, which helps people to sleep cooler.

CHARPOY
(INDIAN SUB-CONTINENT AND SOUTH ASIA)

The **charpoy** is a traditional bed, sometimes called a rope bed. This type of bed has four posts with ropes or fabric tightly woven around and between them. Charpoys are very firm beds and people often sleep on them without a blanket or pillow.

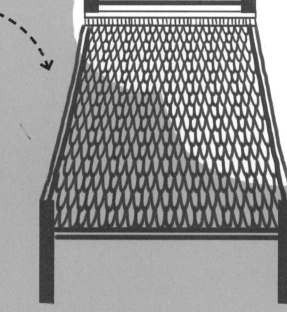

KANG STOVE BED
(CHINA)

Kang stove beds have been used for more than 2,000 years. The kang is a heated platform made of bricks or other materials. Bedding is placed on the platform for a warm place to sleep. During the day, the platform is used for other activities.

FUTON
(JAPAN)

The traditional Japanese bed is the **futon**. A futon has two foldable parts—the mattress and the duvet. A mat called a *tatami* is placed on the floor, and the futon is positioned on top of the mat. Futons can be folded and stored after they are used.

12 | How do animals sleep?

Scientists hesitate to confirm that all animals sleep because of a lack of research on some species. Experts do believe, however, that most animals sleep, and that sleep is as important to their health as it is to ours. But how they sleep is very different across species.

FISH

Scientists aren't certain whether large fish like rays and sharks sleep or just rest. For many other fish, however, there seems to be a difference between being awake and sleeping.

BIRDS

Because some birds can fly for days without stopping, experts used to think that birds could go for days without sleeping. Now, scientists think that birds might be able to sleep *while* they are flying!

INSECTS

Studies have shown that at least some insects need sleep. Indeed, cockroaches and flies can die if they go too long without sleep.

DUCKS IN A ROW

Scientists have found that when ducks sleep in a row on the water, the duck on either end of the row sleeps with one eye open. This allows those ducks to watch for predators.

AMPHIBIANS AND REPTILES

Scientists haven't done a lot of sleep research on these types of animals. However, with the definition of animal sleep now expanding, researchers think that reptiles experience a sleeplike state and amphibians experience a rest phase.

LAND MAMMALS

Research shows that most land mammals sleep. Some experts even think that they can dream.

MARINE MAMMALS

These particular mammals appear to have the ability to sleep with only half of their brain. During this type of sleep, the other half of the brain is awake so they can keep swimming and surface for air.

ALL ABOUT HIBERNATION

Hibernation is often thought of as a seasonal, cold-weather behavior, but there are tropical hibernators, too. In fact, outdoor temperature isn't always the reason animals hibernate; some animals hibernate because of a shortage of food.

Scientists have divided hibernators into two categories: **true hibernators** and **light sleep hibernators**.

True hibernators include groundhogs and ground squirrels. Their state of hibernation is deep and can last longer than 100 days.

Bears and skunks are two animals considered to be light sleep hibernators. They are easily awakened, and their hibernation does not last as long and is not as deep as true hibernators.

SELECT BIBLIOGRAPHY

"Better Sleep for a Better You." Sleep Foundation, n.d. https://www.sleepfoundation.org/.

"Brain Basics: Understanding Sleep." National Institute of Neurological Disorders and Stroke, n.d. https://www.ninds.nih.gov/health-information/public-education/brain-basics/brain-basics-understanding-sleep.

"Circadian Rhythms and Circadian Clock." Centers for Disease Control and Prevention, April 1, 2020. https://www.cdc.gov/niosh/emres/longhourstraining/clock.html.

"Circadian Rhythms." National Institute of General Medical Sciences, n.d. https://nigms.nih.gov/education/fact-sheets/Pages/circadian-rhythms.aspx.

Dubinsky, Dana. "The Connection between Sleep and Growth (Ages 5 to 8)." BabyCenter, n.d. https://www.babycenter.com/child/development/the-connection-between-sleep-and-growth-ages-5-to-8_3658990.

"Facts about Sleep for Parents and School Staff." The Sleep Health Foundation, March 10, 2020. https://www.sleephealthfoundation.org.au/facts-about-sleep-for-parents-and-school-staff.html.

Fliesler, Nancy. "Melatonin for Kids: Is It Effective? Is It Safe?" Boston Children's Answers, June 13, 2022. https://answers.childrenshospital.org/melatonin-for-children.

"How Much Sleep Do I Need?" Centers for Disease Control and Prevention, September 14, 2022. https://www.cdc.gov/sleep/about_sleep/how_much_sleep.html.

Langley, Liz. "These Birds Nap While They Fly—and Other Surprising Ways That Animals Sleep." Animals, November 3, 2021. https://www.nationalgeographic.com/animals/article/surprising-ways-that-animals-sleep.

Leonard, Jayne. "What Is REM Sleep?" Medical News Today, n.d. https://www.medicalnewstoday.com/articles/247927.

Lockett, Eleesha. "Everything to Know About the Stages of Sleep." Healthline, May 30, 2023. https://www.healthline.com/health/healthy-sleep/stages-of-sleep.

MacCutcheon, Megan. "What Is Sleep Hygiene? Hint: It's Not Just Showering Before Bed." GoodTherapy, October 19, 2018. https://www.goodtherapy.org/blog/what-is-sleep-hygiene-hint-its-not-just-showering-before-bed-1019184.

Okoye, Afy. "What Is Sleep?" Sleep Doctor, January 13, 2023. https://thesleepdoctor.com/how-sleep-works/what-is-sleep.

O'Connell, Lindsey. "Who Needs Sleep Anyway?" Do Animals Need to Sleep?, November 1, 2011. https://askabiologist.asu.edu/plosable/who-needs-sleep-anyway.

Phelan, Joe. "What Happens in Your Brain While You Sleep?" LiveScience, October 4, 2022. https://www.livescience.com/what-happens-brain-sleep.

"Sleep." Cleveland Clinic, n.d. https://my.clevelandclinic.org/health/articles/12148-sleep-basics.

"Sleep for Kids—Teaching Kids the Importance of Sleep." Sleep for Kids—Teaching Kids the Importance of Sleep, n.d. http://www.sleepforkids.org/.

Thomson, Chris. "22 Interesting Facts You Didn't Know about Sleep." The Sleep Matters Club, December 21, 2022. https://www.dreams.co.uk/sleep-matters-club/25-facts-about-sleep.

Ullman, Michelle. "The History of the Bed." The Spruce, December 26, 2021. https://www.thespruce.com/the-history-of-the-bed-4062296.

"What Are REM and Non-REM Sleep?" WebMD, n.d. https://www.webmd.com/sleep-disorders/sleep-101.

"What Are Sleep Disorders?" American Psychiatric Association. https://www.psychiatry.org/patients-families/sleep-disorders/what-are-sleep-disorders.

"Why Sleep Matters: Benefits of Sleep." Sleep Medicine, n.d. https://sleep.hms.harvard.edu/education-training/public-education/sleep-and-health-education-program/sleep-health-education-41.